CHRI

in the STC

"This isn't just an attractive book. People who read and pray with it will find it a vehicle of powerful grace—a kind of sacramental for these times."

Msgr. Stephen J. Rossetti
Author of *The Priestly Blessing*

"*Christ in the Storm* is a stunning tribute to one of the most iconic moments in recent history. The prayer of Pope Francis is for every human being and echoes as a timeless call from the heart of Jesus Christ himself."

Sr. Miriam James Heidland, S.O.L.T.
Catholic speaker and author of *Loved as I Am*

"Pope Francis reminds the Church and the world that Jesus was and is with us, and that at the end of the day Christ is all we really need. My prayer is that this book will help us keep our eyes fixed on Jesus, no matter what our situation."

Teresa Tomeo
EWTN radio and television host

"In his message, the Holy Father reminds us that this time of the coronavirus is a call to courage, a call to faith. And as he says, faith does not mean simply agreeing with a set of ideas. Faith means making a decision to entrust our lives to Jesus Christ and to follow his path, to embrace his cross."

Archbishop José Gomez
President of the US Conference of Catholic Bishops

"It was perhaps the most liturgically dramatic moment in the long history of the papacy. This was the pope piloting God's people through a storm like no other."

Austen Ivereigh
Commonweal

"With a wooden crucifix behind him that had been carried through Rome's streets in 1522 against the great plague, Francis sought to bolster faith in a world facing anxiety and fear."

Jason Horowitz
The New York Times

"Pope Francis's lovely *Urbi et Orbi* blessing on March 27 offered the consolation and encouragement we need from our spiritual leaders."

Richard Gaillardetz
Joseph Professor of Catholic Systematic Theology at Boston College and former president of the Catholic Theological Society of America

"In one hour, in one act that millions around the world watched live (and that many more viewed online afterward), Pope Francis, a pastor for the world, reoriented us during his *Urbi et Orbi* blessing. Yes, this world has its complications. But it is not so complicated with Christ. Look to him. Trust in him. For real. If anyone can guide us on our next steps, it is Christ."

Kathryn Jean Lopez
Angelus

"*Christ in the Storm* is more than a coffee table book for Catholics living during COVID-19. In this liturgy celebrated by Pope Francis, and now in this meditation, each of us is invited to a school of devotional prayer—one that may renew parish and family life alike."

From the introduction by **Timothy P. O'Malley**
Director of McGrath Theology Online
McGrath Institute for Church Life at the University of Notre Dame

"Catholicism at its best."

From the foreword by **John L. Allen Jr.**
Vatican expert and editor of *Crux*

CHRIST
in the STORM

An Extraordinary Blessing
for a Suffering World

POPE FRANCIS

Urbi et Orbi, March 27, 2020
Foreword by John L. Allen Jr.
Introduction by Timothy P. O'Malley

AVE MARIA PRESS AVE Notre Dame, Indiana

Foreword © 2020 by John L. Allen Jr.

Introduction © 2020 by Timothy P. O'Malley

Compiled and edited by Jaymie Stuart Wolfe.

© 2020 Ave Maria Press, Inc.

Founded in 1865, Ave Maria Press is a ministry of the United States Province of Holy Cross.

www.avemariapress.com

Hardcover: ISBN-13 978-1-64680-053-7

E-book: ISBN-13 978-1-64680-054-4

Cover design by Katherine Robinson and Kristen Hornyak Bonelli.

Text design by Kristen Hornyak Bonelli.

Printed and bound in the United States of America.

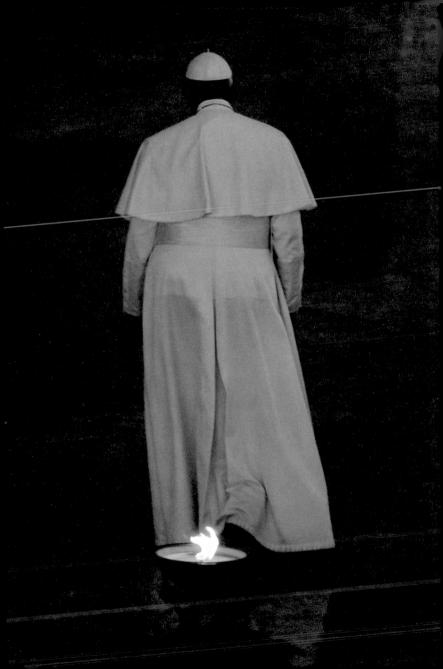

Perhaps it's too early to predict which image from the coronavirus pandemic will prove most iconic around the world, enduring in public consciousness well after the last test has come back negative.

Maybe it'll be the 3-D model of the virus itself, developed by two medical illustrators at the Centers for Disease Control to look both accurate and menacing. Perhaps it'll be the facemask or, grimmer still, the body bag. It's also possible it'll end up being shuttered businesses and twenty-first century bread lines, especially if the next act in the drama is a lasting global recession.

In Italy, however, and above all in the city of Rome, no such speculation is necessary. It's already crystal-clear which image Romans will take with them to their graves from this calamity, and it carries a precise date, time, and location: March 27, 6:00 p.m. Rome time, in St. Peter's Square.

It was then that Pope Francis delivered perhaps the most extraordinary blessing in the long history of the papacy, offering a surprise benediction *Urbi et Orbi*—"To the City and the World"—in the midst of the agony of the pandemic.

Fifty years from now, if you were to ask a Roman to close his or her eyes and give you the first thing that comes to mind when you say the word "coronavirus," it would almost certainly be a memory of Pope Francis standing alone in that usually overflowing square, flanked by the images of *Maria Salus Populi Romani* and the miraculous crucifix of San Marcello, his voice carrying out through the rain to an eerily silent city, punctuated only by the harrowing sound of ambulance sirens passing by.

The Vatican has always had a keen sense of drama, but never were those instincts more finely tuned than on that remarkable Friday night. Aldo Grasso, Italy's best-known media historian and theorist, described the moment.

"One day we'll remember these sad times we're living with many other images: the daily count of the dead, the lines at the hospitals, the frantic challenge to an invisible enemy," Grasso wrote. "But the prayer for the end of the pandemic, the solemn *Urbi et Orbi* blessing, the solitude of the pope, will end up as one of those decisive moments in which television captures our history, our anguish, in real time."

"The wind that blew the pages of the Gospels during the funeral of John Paul II, or the helicopter ride of Pope Benedict when he resigned, both moved us, but they're nothing in comparison to the shock of seeing the empty square surrounded by the colonnade of Bernini," Grasso continued.

The pope's language that night seemed to give voice to the national mood. Translation doesn't quite do it justice, straining to capture the poetry of the Italian original, but probably the most oft-cited phrasing came near the beginning.

"Thick darkness has gathered over our squares, our streets and our cities; it has taken over our lives, filling everything with a deafening silence and a distressing void, which stops everything as it passes by," the pope said. "We feel it in the air, we notice in people's gestures, their glances give them away. We find ourselves afraid and lost."

The heart of Francis's argument was that the disciples too felt fear, and the antidote lies in Christ and the promise of the resurrection as Easter approaches. It was a message of hope, directed especially at Italians, who were reeling because the country had set a new record for deaths in the previous 24 hours, losing an astonishing 969 people in one day.

"We've become aware that we're all in the same boat," the pope said, "all fragile and disoriented, but at the same time important and necessary, all called to remain together, all needing to comfort each other in turn."

One measure of the impact of the moment is this: Of the roughly 27 million Italians (out of a total national population of 70 million) who were watching television that evening, according to the national ratings service Auditel, a stunning 17.4 million, or 64.6 percent, were tuned into the pope's address. That makes the *Ubi et Orbi* the highest rated broadcast in the history of Italian television, beating out even the mammoth numbers for the acclaimed annual pop music festival at San Remo.

Since the square was closed even to journalists, my wife and I were members of that vast TV audience. I confess I came to the broadcast with a cluttered mind and mostly out of a sense of duty, since the main Catholic storyline at the time seemed to be an internal debate over whether the Church should assent to the suspension of sacramental life being decreed by a growing number of governments around the world. It was an acrimonious back-and-forth which, in some ways, reflected the deeper tensions unleashed by the Francis papacy between progressive reformers and defenders of tradition.

Yet that night, Francis reminded me of the transcendent capacities of the papacy.

For a moment, he lifted me and everyone else out of the political arena, out of the climate of fear and frustration imposed by the pandemic, and he reminded us all of the inexhaustible power of a hope rooted in faith. Even Italian friends who are anti-clerical to the core told me they wept at what they saw and heard, sensing that someone, at long last, had approached this calamity in the proper key—not principally as an administrative or technical challenge but as a shock to the soul.

Francis, that night, became the whole world's pastor, beginning with his own flock as the Bishop of Rome and radiating out to the entire "*orbi*."

That evening of March 27 was haunting, evocative, unforgettable, and, in all the ways that really matter, Catholicism at its best. These pages are a precious contribution to enshrining that moment in the collective memory, where it deserves a pride of place, perhaps especially for those who didn't have the good fortune to be in Rome, as we did, to watch history unfold before our eyes.

INTRODUCTION
Timothy P. O'Malley

Early in his pontificate, Pope Francis taught us that evangelization "has to concentrate on the essentials, on what is most beautiful, most grand, most appealing and at the same time most necessary" (*The Joy of the Gospel*, 35). On March 27, 2020, with the world immersed in a pandemic, Pope Francis in the name of Jesus Christ blessed the city of Rome and the world in a liturgy that manifested what was most beautiful, most grand, most appealing, and most necessary for Catholics and the human family as a whole. In a windy St. Peter's Square, Pope Francis held up to a suffering world the image of Jesus and our Blessed Mother, the crucifixion of our Lord, and his eucharistic presence. The human voice cried out for the intervention of the crucified and risen Lord through poetic hymns and chants. And the whole world listened to the preaching of an octogenarian Argentinian pope in an empty St. Peter's Square, reminding us that Christ was still present among us in the storm of life.

This book offers a meditation on the liturgy of this remarkable day in the history of the Church. The temptation, of course, is to treat a compilation like this as a mere commemoration of what took place in March in the age of the coronavirus. But this volume is something more than a coffee-table book for Catholics living during COVID-19. It is an invitation to remember practices, images, and chants that are most beautiful, most essential, most necessary for Catholic life. In the end, COVID-19 is a reminder of the brevity and precariousness of life, a remembering of death that has been integral to the Christian faithful since the early Church. Our forebears in faith knew how to face death with hope. In this text, we will be invited to remember those devotional practices that can sustain us not just in a pandemic but as we traverse through this "valley of tears" under the protection of our Lord and his Blessed Mother. In this liturgy celebrated by Pope Francis, and now this meditation, each of us is invited to a school of devotional prayer—one that may renew parish and family life alike.

*L*ex orandi, lex credenda: "the law of prayer is the law of belief." In other words, if you want to know what the Church believes, listen to how she prays. If ever an occasion clearly demonstrated this truth, it was the extraordinary *Urbi et Orbi* on March 27, 2020. Billed as a "moment of prayer," the event was not only a deeply spiritual response to a world in crisis watched by millions. It was also a portrait of the Church at her best—the Mystical Body of Christ in the world, offering healing and hope. As such, its value extends far beyond the crisis that inspired it.

But the *Urbi et Orbi* holy hour was also something else: a representation of the essentials of Catholic faith and practice. Watching the event with a few family members, I found myself adding to the necessarily abbreviated broadcast commentary to explain the significance of what we were witnessing as the Church drew beautifully from two thousand years of sacred tradition. All the hallmarks of Catholic faith were engaged: Scripture, authoritative teaching, Marian devotion, veneration of the Cross, an icon, a crucifix with a tradition of miraculous grace, penitential acts, intercessory prayer, eucharistic adoration, the mercy of a plenary indulgence, and praise. In short, the hour was an experience of Catholicism in miniature.

Christ in the Storm walks readers through each of these facets of Catholic Christianity as they unfolded in this extraordinary and historic event, but not merely for the sake of historical record. Like all prayer, the extraordinary *Urbi et Orbi* holy hour is timeless. It can become a well to which we return often: a master class in the "school of devotion," a framework for deepening personal prayer.

To that end, this book contains the texts of all the readings, teachings, prayers, and chants offered, accompanied by valuable historical information, brief presentations of spiritual significance and liturgical context, and stirringly beautiful color photographs from the event. Those curious about the faith, as well as practicing (and nonpracticing) Catholics, will find in these pages something to treasure, something worth taking with them into the future, and an ongoing source of comfort and hope as we face the challenges that lie ahead.

We do not face life's tragedies alone. The suffering we all encounter at one time or another can bring us not only to our knees but also to the beating heart of the living God. No matter who you are or what your storm is, the Catholic Church wants you to know that Christ is with you in the midst of it all.

Jaymie Stuart Wolfe, Compiler and Editor
June 1, 2020, Memorial of the Blessed Virgin
Mary, Mother of the Church

While popes have always given blessings, the *Urbi et Orbi* ("to the city and the world") has special significance as the most solemn form of papal blessing. The blessing dates back to the period of the Roman Empire when the words *urbis et orbis* were first used in the title of the Basilica of St. John Lateran. Originally built in the fourth century during the reign of the emperor Constantine, the first cathedral of Rome has been known as "the mother and head of all churches in the city and the world" (*omnium urbis et orbis ecclesiarum mater et caput*).

For many centuries the blessing was imparted from St. John Lateran as well as from several of the more prominent churches of Rome during various holy days throughout the year. In modern times,

Urbi et Orbi blessings occur on Christmas, Easter, and just after a papal election. They are usually given from the central *loggia,* or balcony, of St. Peter's Basilica at noon. The pope speaks briefly and concludes his address with greetings in numerous languages to the throngs that fill St. Peter's Square. Traditionally attached to the blessing is an opportunity for the faithful to gain a plenary indulgence.

The extraordinary *Urbi et Orbi* on March 27, 2020 was unique. It was held at dusk and at the doors of St. Peter's Basilica opened to an empty square. Pope Francis did not use the traditional form of the Apostolic Blessing, but rather the Rite of Eucharistic Benediction. As with all *Urbi et Orbi* blessings, the event created an opportunity for the pope to address Catholics not only in the city of Rome but also scattered throughout the world.

The Bible is the Word of God and Catholics reverence it as such. This gospel was chosen to bring both encouragement and hope to the world in a time of darkness, uncertainty, and fear.

On that day, when evening had come, he said to them, "Let us go across to the other side." And leaving the crowd behind, they took him with them in the boat, just as he was. Other boats were with him. A great windstorm arose, and the waves beat into the boat, so that the boat was already being swamped. But he was in the stern, asleep on the cushion; and they woke him up and said to him, "Teacher, do you not care that we are perishing?" He woke up and rebuked the wind, and said to the sea, "Peace! Be still!" Then the wind ceased, and there was a dead calm. He said to them, "Why are you afraid? Have you still no faith?" And they were filled with great awe and said to one another, "Who then is this, that even the wind and the sea obey him?"

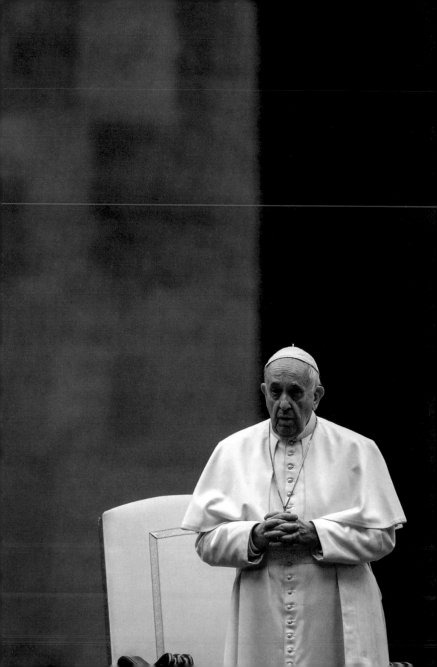

HOMILY BY POPE FRANCIS

The pope has many official titles. Among them are Successor of Peter, Bishop of Rome, Vicar of Christ, Supreme Pontiff of the Universal Church, Sovereign of the Vatican City State, and Servant of the Servants of God. While we often see the papacy as the highest position of leadership and power in the Church, it is more accurately understood as the office of shepherd and teacher of all Christians. All bishops are the successors of the original apostles. When the pope preaches, he is exercising the teaching office, known as the magisterium, of the Church.

When evening had come" (Mk 4:35). The gospel passage we have just heard begins like this. For weeks now it has been evening. Thick darkness has gathered over our squares, our streets and our cities; it has taken over our lives, filling everything with a deafening silence and a distressing void, that stops everything as it passes by; we feel it in the air, we notice in people's gestures, their glances give them away. We find ourselves afraid and lost. Like the disciples in the gospel we were caught off guard by an unexpected, turbulent storm. We have realized that we are on the same boat, all of us fragile and disoriented, but at the same time important and needed, all of us called to row together, each of us in need of comforting the other. On this boat . . . are all of us. Just like those disciples, who spoke anxiously with one voice, saying "We are perishing" (v. 38), so we too have realized that we cannot go on thinking of ourselves, but only together can we do this.

It is easy to recognize ourselves in this story. What is harder to understand is Jesus' attitude. While his disciples are quite naturally alarmed and desperate, he stands in the stern, in the part of the boat that sinks first. And what does he do? In spite of the tempest, he sleeps on soundly, trusting in the

Father; this is the only time in the gospels we see Jesus sleeping. When he wakes up, after calming the wind and the waters, he turns to the disciples in a reproaching voice: "Why are you afraid? Have you no faith?" (v. 40).

Let us try to understand. In what does the lack of the disciples' faith consist, as contrasted with Jesus' trust? They had not stopped believing in him; in fact, they called on him. But we see how they call on him: "Teacher, do you not care if we perish?" (v. 38). Do you not care: they think that Jesus is not interested in them, does not care about them. One of the things that hurts us and our families most when we hear it said is: "Do you not care about me?" It is a phrase that wounds and unleashes storms in our hearts. It would have shaken Jesus too. Because he, more than anyone, cares about us. Indeed, once they have called on him, he saves his disciples from their discouragement.

The storm exposes our vulnerability and uncovers those false and superfluous certainties around which we have constructed our daily schedules, our projects, our habits, and priorities. It shows us how we have allowed to become dull and feeble the very things that nourish, sustain, and strengthen our lives and our communities. The tempest lays bare all our prepackaged ideas and forgetfulness of what nourishes our people's souls; all those attempts that anesthetize us with ways of thinking and acting that supposedly "save" us, but instead prove incapable of putting us in touch with our roots and keeping alive the memory of those who have gone before us. We deprive ourselves of the antibodies we need to confront adversity.

In this storm, the façade of those stereotypes with which we camouflaged our egos, always worrying about our image, has fallen away, uncovering once more that (blessed) common belonging, of which we cannot be deprived: our belonging as brothers and sisters.

"Why are you afraid? Have you no faith?" Lord, your word this evening strikes us and regards us, all of us. In this world, that you love more than we do, we have gone ahead at breakneck speed, feeling powerful and able to do anything. Greedy for profit, we let ourselves get caught up in things, and lured away by haste. We did not stop at your reproach to us, we were not shaken awake by wars or injustice across the world, nor did we listen to the cry of the poor or of our ailing planet. We carried on regardless, thinking we would stay healthy in a world that was sick. Now that we are in a stormy sea, we implore you: "Wake up, Lord!"

"Why are you afraid? Have you no faith?" Lord, you are calling to us, calling us to faith. Which is not so much believing that you exist, but coming to you and trusting in you. This Lent your call reverberates urgently: "Be converted!", "Return to me with all your heart" (Jl 2:12). You are calling on us to seize this time of trial as a time of choosing. It is not the time of your judgement, but of our judgement: a time to choose what matters and what passes away, a time to separate what is necessary from what is not. It is a time to get our lives back on track with regard to you, Lord, and to others. We can look to so many exemplary companions for the journey, who, even though fearful, have reacted by giving their lives. This is the force of the Spirit poured out and fashioned in courageous and generous self-denial. It is the life in the Spirit that can redeem, value and demonstrate how our lives are woven together and sustained by ordinary people—often forgotten people—who do not appear in newspaper and magazine headlines nor on the grand catwalks of the latest show, but who without any doubt are in these very days writing the decisive events of our time: doctors, nurses, supermarket employees, cleaners, caregivers, providers of transport, law and order forces, volunteers, priests, religious men and women, and so very many others who have understood that no one reaches salvation by themselves. In the face of so much suffering, where the authentic development of our peoples is assessed, we experience the priestly prayer of Jesus: "That they may all be one" (Jn 17:21). How many people every day are exercising patience and offering hope, taking care to sow not panic but a shared responsibility. How many fathers, mothers, grandparents, and teachers are showing our children, in small everyday gestures, how to face up to and navigate a crisis by adjusting their routines, lifting their gaze, and fostering prayer. How many are praying, offering, and interceding for the good of all. Prayer and quiet service: these are our victorious weapons.

"Why are you afraid? Have you no faith?" Faith begins when we realize we are in need of salvation. We are not self-sufficient; by ourselves we founder: we need the Lord, like ancient navigators needed the stars. Let us invite Jesus into the boats of our lives. Let us hand over our fears to him so that he can conquer them. Like the disciples, we will experience that with him on board there will be no shipwreck. Because this is God's strength: turning to the good everything that happens to us, even the bad things. He brings serenity into our storms, because with God life never dies.

The Lord asks us and, in the midst of our tempest, invites us to reawaken and put into practice that solidarity and hope capable of giving strength, support and meaning to these hours when everything seems to be floundering. The Lord awakens so as to reawaken and revive our Easter faith. We have an anchor: by his Cross we have been saved. We have a rudder: by his Cross we have been redeemed. We have a hope: by his Cross we have been healed and embraced so that nothing and no one can separate us from his redeeming love. In the midst of isolation when we are suffering from a lack of tenderness and chances to meet up, and we experience the loss of so many things, let us once again listen to the proclamation that saves us: he is risen and is living by our side. The Lord asks us from his Cross to rediscover the life that awaits us, to look towards those who look to us, to strengthen, recognize and foster the grace that lives within us. Let us not quench the wavering flame (cf. Is 42:3) that never falters, and let us allow hope to be rekindled.

Embracing his Cross means finding the courage to embrace all the hardships of the present time, abandoning for a moment our eagerness for power and possessions in order to make room for the creativity that only the Spirit is capable of inspiring. It means finding the courage to create spaces where everyone can recognize that they are called, and to allow new forms of hospitality, fraternity, and solidarity. By his Cross we have been saved in order to embrace hope and let it strengthen and sustain all measures and all possible avenues for helping us protect ourselves and others. Embracing the Lord in order to embrace hope: that is the strength of faith, which frees us from fear and gives us hope.

"Why are you afraid? Have you no faith?" Dear brothers and sisters, from this place that tells of Peter's rock-solid faith, I would like this evening to entrust all of you to the Lord, through the intercession of Mary, Health of the People and Star of the stormy Sea. From this colonnade that embraces Rome and the whole world, may God's blessing come down upon you as a consoling embrace. Lord, may you bless the world, give health to our bodies, and comfort our hearts. You ask us not to be afraid. Yet our faith is weak and we are fearful. But you, Lord, will not leave us at the mercy of the storm. Tell us again: "Do not be afraid" (Mt 28:5). And we, together with Peter, "cast all our anxieties onto you, for you care about us" (cf. 1 Pt 5:7).

THE ICON OF
Maria Salus Populi Romani

The origin of this treasured icon of Mary and the infant Jesus is clouded in legend. Measuring five feet high and over three feet wide, the image has long been attributed to St. Luke. According to one legend, the Christian women of Jerusalem prevailed upon the evangelist to paint a portrait of the Blessed Virgin Mary and that he did so as he listened to Mary's recollections of her Son's early life. The thick cedar plank on which the icon is painted is reputedly the top of a wooden table built by the young Jesus.

How and when the image arrived in Rome also remains uncertain. Some believe that the icon remained in Jerusalem until St. Helen, the mother of Constantine the Great, discovered it. Others speak of its arrival in Rome from Crete during the pontificate of Gregory the Great. For centuries, the icon has been kept at the Basilica of Santa Maria Maggiore (St. Mary Major), a fifth-century basilica that is the oldest church in the West dedicated to Mary. Dating for the image varies widely and is complicated by the fact that additional layers have been painted over the original work. Restoration of the icon was completed in 2018.

This image has been credited with special graces and miracles, and many popes have made recourse to its veneration in times of crisis. It is said that Pope Gregory the Great carried it throughout Rome during the Easter season in 593 seeking the intercession of Mary for an end to the "Plague of Justinian" at that time. When the plague quickly receded, the image was given its lasting title: *Salus Populi Romani*—"Protectress and Health of the Roman People." In 1571, Pope Pius V venerated the icon to pray for a victory over Muslim forces at the Battle of Lepanto. Pope Gregory XVI honored the image during an epidemic of cholera in 1837. Pope Francis has visited this icon before and after every apostolic journey and for every Marian feast.

It is important to note that while sacred art is a rich part of Catholic tradition, Catholics do not worship icons, paintings, or statues. Instead, an image is used to honor the person it represents. The Church holds that the Blessed Virgin Mary is preeminent among the saints because she was chosen by God to be the mother of the Savior. We ask the intercession of Mary just as we ask our friends and family members to pray for us. We do so, remembering that the first public miracle Jesus performed—at the wedding in Cana—was at the request of his mother.

MARIAN DEVOTION:
Sub Tuum Praesidium

The Church loves the Blessed Virgin Mary and has always expressed that love in prayer. Catholics look to Mary as the model of Christian discipleship and trust that she will lead them to her Son, Jesus. We turn to Mary, believing that her role as mother did not cease at the end of her earthly life but extends to all of us, both as individuals and as the universal Church. In the Sub Tuum Praesidium *(which translates to "under your protection"), we seek Mary's motherly protection and care. It is the oldest known hymn to Mary and is preserved on a papyrus dating from the third century.*

Under Your Protection

Under your protection we flee, holy Mother of God. Despise not our petitions in our needs, but deliver us always from all dangers, O glorious and blessed Virgin. Amen.

Sub Tuum Praesidium

Sub tuum praesidium confugimus, sancta Dei Genetrix. Nostras deprecationes ne despicias in necessitatibus, sed a periculis cunctis libera nos semper, Virgo gloriosa et benedicta. Amen.

The Miraculous Crucifix was brought from the church of San Marcello al Corso to St. Peter's Square the day before the extraordinary *Urbi et Orbi*. The large wooden crucifix dates from the late fourteenth century. Prior to 1519, the crucifix hung in the Oratory of the Most Holy Crucifix. The church caught fire on May 22–23 of that year and was completely destroyed. When people rushed to the building at dawn, they found the crucifix intact above the altar, however, still lit by oil lamps.

In 1522, just a few years after the fire, the city of Rome suffered a terrible outbreak of the Black Plague. Remembering how the crucifix had been preserved, friars of the Servants of Mary carried it through the streets from San Marcello al Corso to St. Peter's Square. The procession stopped in each quarter of the city and lasted sixteen days. When the crucifix was returned to San Marcello, the plague had disappeared from Rome completely.

Since then, the Miraculous Crucifix has been processed to St. Peter's Square during every Roman Holy Year, generally occurring about every fifty years. The back of the crucifix is engraved with the name of each pope who reigned during those processions. Prior to the extraordinary *Urbi et Orbi*, the most recent event involving the Miraculous Crucifix was St. John Paul II's "Day of Forgiveness" during the Jubilee Year of 2000. The crucifix was kept at St. Peter's after the *Urbi et Orbi*, remaining present for all the liturgies of Holy Week.

The Miraculous Crucifix is unique, but every crucifix reminds us that God has answered prayers in times of crisis before, and that the sorrows we endure can be meaningful when united to the sacrificial death of Christ. Jesus knows what it is to suffer: to be treated unjustly, to be rejected and abandoned, to experience the desperation of terrible pain, and even death. Adversity does not distance us from God; he is with us in our distress. When we embrace the Cross, we invite the Savior into our pain and more deeply embrace his love for us.

VENERATION
OF THE CROSS:
Adoramus Te, Christe

While the Cross is a symbol of suffering, it is also the sign of our redemption. This prayer is part of the traditional Stations of the Cross devotion. Here, it was sung during the Holy Father's act of veneration on behalf of the whole Church. The Church honors the Cross, the instrument of Christ's sacrificial death, because it is also the source of our salvation and hope. In Christ crucified, we know that the Lord is with us when we suffer.

We Adore You, O Christ

We adore you, O Christ,
and we bless you,
because by your cross
you have redeemed the world.

Adoramus Te, Christe

Adoramus te, Christe,
et benedicimus tibi,
quia per crucem tuam
redemisti mundum.

A PLEA
FOR GOD'S MERCY:
Parce Domine

The refrain of this prayer for mercy comes from Joel 2:17. The Parce Domine *is traditionally prayed during the penitential season of Lent. It is offered with confidence in God's mercy and in the hope that our sins, though many, will be forgiven.*

Spare Us, O Lord

Spare us, O Lord, spare us, your people:
do not be angry with us forever.
Let us bow before the vindicating wrath;
Let us weep before the Judge;
Let our mouths cry out with supplication,
Let us all speak, falling prostrate:
Spare us, O Lord, spare us, your people:
do not be angry with us forever.
O God, our evil has offended
Your forbearance;
O Forgiving One,
Pour forth on us your pardon from above.
Spare us, O Lord, spare us, your people:
do not be angry with us forever.
Giving to us an acceptable time,
Grant that in the rivers of our tears

Parce Domine

Parce Domine, parce populo tuo:
ne in aeternum irascaris nobis.
Flectamus iram vindicem,
Ploremus ante Iudicem;
Clamemus ore supplici,
Dicamus omnes cernui:
Parce Domine, parce populo tuo:
ne in aeternum irascaris nobis.
Nostris malis offendimus
Tuam Deus clementiam
Effunde nobis desuper
Remissor indulgentiam.
Parce Domine, parce populo tuo:
ne in aeternum irascaris nobis.
Dans tempus acceptablie,
Da lacrimarum rivulis

The sacrifice of our hearts is cleansed,
Enkindled by joyful charity.

Spare us, O Lord, spare us, your people:
do not be angry with us forever.

Hear, good Creator,
Our prayers with tears
Poured out in this holy fast
Of forty days.

Spare us, O Lord, spare us, your people:
do not be angry with us forever.

O kind Searcher of hearts,
You know the weakness of our strength;
To those returning to you,
Show the grace of forgiveness.

Spare us, O Lord, spare us, your people:
do not be angry with us forever.

Lavare cordis victimam,
Quam laeta adurat caritas.
Parce Domine, parce populo tuo:
ne in aeternum irascaris nobis.
Audi, benigne Conditor,
Nostras preces cum fletibus
In hoc sacro ieiunio,
Fusas quadragenario.
Parce Domine, parce populo tuo:
ne in aeternum irascaris nobis.
Scrutator alme cordium,
Infirma tu cis virium;
Ad te reversis exhibe
Remissionis gratiam.
Parce Domine, parce populo tuo:
ne in aeternum irascaris nobis.

EUCHARISTIC ADORATION:
Adoro Te Devote

The Real Presence of Christ in the Eucharist has been a tenet of Christian faith from the beginning. Because Catholics believe the consecrated Host is the Body, Blood, Soul, and Divinity of Jesus Christ, we also believe that it is worthy of all adoration and praise. While the Eucharist is usually reserved in a tabernacle under lock and key, it is also publicly exposed in a monstrance or ostensorium for the purpose of prayer and devotion.

The Adoro Te Devote *is among the collection of eucharistic hymns written by Thomas Aquinas in the thirteenth century. This prayer ushers in a time of silence in which we are invited to open ourselves to the Real Presence of the risen Christ in the Eucharist, express our love for him, and listen to God in the sanctuary of our hearts.*

Hidden God, Devoutly I Adore

Hidden God, devoutly I adore you,
Truly present underneath these veils:
All my heart subdues itself before you,
Since it all before you faints and fails.

Not to sight, or taste, or touch be credit
Hearing only do we trust secure;
I believe, for God the Son has said it—
Word of truth that ever shall endure.

On the Cross was veiled your divine splendor,
Here humanity lies hidden too;
Unto both alike my faith I render,
As implored the contrite thief, I sue.

Though I look not on your wounds with
    Thomas,
You, my Lord, and you, my God, I call:

Adoro Te Devote

Adoro te devote, latens deitas,
Quae sub his figuris vere latitas;
Tibi se cor meum totum subiicit,
Quia te contemplans totum deficit.

Visus, tactus, gustus in te fallitur,
Sed auditu solo tuto creditur.
Credo quidquid dixit Dei Filius;
Nil hoc verbo Veritatis verius.

In Cruce latebat sola Deitas,
At hic latet simul et Humanitas,
Ambo tamen credens atque confitens,
Peto quod petivit latro poenitens.

Plagas, sicut Thomas, non intueor:

Deum tamen meum te confiteor.

Make me more and more believe your
    promise,
Hope in you, and love you over all.

O memorial of my Savior dying,
Living Bread, that gives life to man;
Make my soul, its life from you supplying,
Taste your sweetness, as on earth it can.

Grant, O Jesus, Pelican of heaven,
Me, a sinner, in your Blood to bathe,
To a single drop of which is given
All the world from all its sin to save.

Contemplating, Lord, your hidden presence,
Grant me what I thirst for and implore,
In the revelation of your essence
To behold your glory evermore.
Amen.

Fac me tibi semper magis credere,

In te spem habere, te diligere.

O memoriale mortis Domini,
Panis vivus, vitam praestans homini,
Praesta meae menti de te vivere,
Et te illi semper dulce sapere.

Pie Pelicane, Iesu Domine,
Me immundum munda tuo Sanguine:
Cuius una stilla salvum facere
Totum mundum quit ab omni scelere.

Iesu, quem velatum nunc aspicio,
Oro, fiat illud quod tam sitio:
Ut te revelata cernens facie,
Visu sim beatus tuae gloriae.
Amen.

The word "litany" comes from a Greek word meaning "to implore or entreat." This form of prayer is characterized by a number of invocations or petitions offered by a leader and followed by the repetition of a congregational response. Litanies have been used in both Jewish and Christian prayer traditions, especially in conjunction with public processions during times of war, plague, or natural disaster. Like the one below, many litanies have focused their petitions on the forgiveness of sins and community welfare; others are more devotional in nature.

The Scriptures teach us that God is a loving Father and encourage us to bring our needs to him. As St. Peter wrote, "Cast all your anxieties on him, for he cares about you" (1 Pt 5:7). The whole Church gathers before the light of Christ's eucharistic presence and asks for God's help.

Litany of Supplication

We adore you, O Lord.

True God and true man, truly present in this
holy Sacrament,

We adore you, O Lord.

Our Savior, God with us, faithful and rich in
mercy,

We adore you, O Lord.

King and Lord of creation and of history,

We adore you, O Lord.

Conqueror of sin and death,

We adore you, O Lord.

Friend of humankind, the Risen One, the
Living One who sits at the right hand of the
Father,

We adore you, O Lord.

We believe in you, O Lord.

Only begotten Son of the Father, descended
from heaven for our salvation,

We believe in you, O Lord.

Heavenly physician, who bows down over our
misery,

We believe in you, O Lord.

Lamb who was slain, who offer yourself to
rescue us from evil,

We believe in you, O Lord.

Good Shepherd, who gives your life for the
flock which you love,

We believe in you, O Lord.

Living bread and medicine for immortality,
who give us eternal life,

We believe in you, O Lord.

Deliver us, O Lord.

From the power of Satan and the seductions of
the world,

Deliver us, O Lord.

From the pride and presumption of being able
to do anything without you,

Deliver us, O Lord.

From the deceptions of fear and anxiety,

Deliver us, O Lord.

From unbelief and desperation,

Deliver us, O Lord.

From hardness of heart and the incapacity to
love,

Deliver us, O Lord.

Save us, O Lord.

From every evil that afflicts humanity,

Save us, O Lord.

From hunger, from famine, and from egoism,

Save us, O Lord.

From illnesses, epidemics, and the fear of our
brothers and sisters,

Save us, O Lord.

From devastating madness, from ruthless
interests, and from violence,

Save us, O Lord.

From being deceived, from false information,
and the manipulation of consciences,

Save us, O Lord.

Comfort us, O Lord.

Protect your Church which crosses the desert,

Comfort us, O Lord.

Protect humanity terrified by fear and anguish,

Comfort us, O Lord.

Protect the sick and the dying, oppressed by
loneliness,

Comfort us, O Lord.

Protect doctors and healthcare providers
exhausted by the difficulties they are facing,

Comfort us, O Lord.

Protect politicians and decision makers
who bear the weight of having to make
decisions,

Comfort us, O Lord.

Grant us your Spirit, O Lord.

In the hour of trial and from confusion,

Grant us your Spirit, O Lord.

In temptation and in our fragility,

Grant us your Spirit, O Lord.

In the battle against evil and sin,

Grant us your Spirit, O Lord.

In the search for what is truly good and true joy,

Grant us your Spirit, O Lord.

In the decision to remain in you and in your friendship,

Grant us your Spirit, O Lord.

Open us to hope, O Lord.

Should sin oppress us,

Open us to hope, O Lord.

Should hatred close our hearts,

Open us to hope, O Lord.

Should sorrow visit us,

Open us to hope, O Lord.

Should indifference cause us anguish,

Open us to hope, O Lord.
Should death overwhelm us,
Open us to hope, O Lord.

BENEDICTION OF THE MOST BLESSED SACRAMENT:
Tantum Ergo

The Tantum Ergo *comes from a eucharistic hymn* (Pange Lingua) *written by St. Thomas Aquinas. Originally composed for the first Solemnity of Corpus Christi, which was instituted by Pope Urban IV in 1264, this hymn is chanted at the end of the liturgy on Holy Thursday as well as throughout the year at Exposition and Benediction of the Most Blessed Sacrament. In this way, adoration of the Eucharist is tangibly linked to the Last Supper and Christ's institution of the Sacrament of his Body and Blood.*

Down in Adoration Falling

Down in adoration falling,
Here the sacred Host we hail,
Over ancient forms departing
Newer rites of grace prevail;
Faith for all defects supplying,
Where the feeble senses fail.

To the everlasting Father,
And the Son who reigns on high,
With the Holy Spirit proceeding
Forth from each eternally,
Be salvation, honor, blessing,
Might and endless majesty.
Amen.
V. You have given them bread from heaven.
R. Having within it all sweetness.
Let us pray:

Tantum Ergo

Tantum ergo Sacramentum
Veneremur cernui,
Et antiquum documentum
Novo cedat ritui;
Praestet fides supplementum
Sensuum defectui.

Genitori, Genitoque
Laus et iubilatio,
Salus, honor, virtus quoque
Sit et benedictio:
procedenti ab utroque
Compar sit laudatio.
Amen.
V. Panem de caelo praestitisti eis.
R. Omne delectamentum in se habentem.
Oremus:

Lord Jesus Christ, who in this wonderful
Sacrament have left us a memorial of your
Passion: grant us, we pray, so to revere the
sacred mysteries of your Body and Blood, that
we may always to be conscious of the fruits
of your redemption. You, who live and reign
forever and ever.
Amen.

Domine Jesu Christe, qui nobis sub
Sacramento mirabili, passionis tuae
memoriam reliquisti: tribue, quaesumus, ita
nos Corporis et Sanguinis tui sacra mysteria
venerari, ut redemptionis tuae fructum in
nobis iugiter sentiamus. Qui vivis et regnas in
saecula saeculorum.

Amen.

PAPAL AND EUCHARISTIC BLESSING

Two different types of blessing were brought together at the extraordinary *Urbi et Orbi*: the papal blessing and the eucharistic blessing. Exposition of the Holy Eucharist often concludes with the Rite of Benediction during which the Sign of the Cross is made by an ordained minister with the monstrance. This is what Pope Francis did instead of extending the customary Apostolic Blessing as the successor of St. Peter. Carrying the monstrance just outside the doors of of the basilica, the Holy Father imparted the silent and solemn blessing of Christ Jesus to the city and the world. The Church continually seeks to bring Christ to the world as it is, and entrusts all creation can and will be to his loving care.

Pope Francis offered a plenary indulgence to all who participated in this extraordinary *Urbi et Orbi*, including those who did so through various forms of communications media or simply through the desire to participate spiritually. Under the circumstances at the time, the usual conditions of sacramental Confession and Holy Communion were not required.

While God forgives our sins through the Sacrament of Reconciliation, the sacrament does not eliminate any chastisement or ongoing purification that occurs during our earthly lives or after death in purgatory. A plenary indulgence is the remission of all temporal punishment due to sin. That is, it frees a person from the suffering that would normally occur as the result of sinfulness. A plenary indulgence is a gift of God's abundant mercy, which he offers to us through Christ and his Church.

THE DIVINE PRAISES:
Laudes Divinae

The Divine Praises were written in Italian in 1797 by Jesuit priest Luigi Felici. They were first intended as a prayer of reparation for the sins of blasphemy and profanity. Today, the Divine Praises are most often offered during Benediction of the Most Blessed Sacrament. Whenever we praise God, we join our voices to the unceasing and eternal praise of the angels and saints in heaven.

The Divine Praises

Blessed be God.

Blessed be his Holy Name.

Blessed be Jesus Christ, true God and true man.

Blessed be the Name of Jesus.

Blessed be his most sacred Heart.

Blessed be his most precious Blood.

Blessed be Jesus in the most holy Sacrament of the altar.

Blessed be the Holy Spirit, the Paraclete.

Blessed be the great Mother of God, Mary most holy.

Blessed be her holy and Immaculate Conception.

Blessed be her glorious Assumption.

Laudes Divinae

Benedictus Deus.

Benedictum Nomen Sanctum eius.

Benedictus Iesus Christus, verus Deus et verus homo.

Benedictum Nomen Iesu.

Benedictum Cor eius sacratissimum.

Benedictus Sanguis eius pretiosissimus.

Benedictus Iesus in sanctissimo altaris Sacramento.

Benedictus Sanctus Spiritus, Paraclitus.

Benedicta excelsa Mater Dei, Maria sanctissima.

Benedicta sancta eius et Immaculata Conceptio.

Benedicta eius gloriosa Assumptio.

Blessed be the name of Mary, Virgin and
Mother.
Blessed be St. Joseph, her most chaste Spouse.

Blessed be God in his angels, and in his saints.

Amen.

Benedictum nomen Mariae, Virginis et Matris.

Benedictus sanctus Ioseph, eius castissimus
    Sponsus.
Benedictus Deus in angelis suis, et in sanctis
    suis.
Amen.

REPOSE OF THE EUCHARIST:
Laudate Dominum

The Holy Hour concluded with the chanting of Psalm 117, the Laudate Dominum. *Although the Holy Eucharist is reposed in the tabernacle, Christ remains with us. Even when we do not see him, even when we cannot receive Holy Communion, he is with us always. The Eucharist, the Presence of the living God, is the greatest treasure held in our churches. It is what makes them truly houses of God.*

While we thank God for all he has done for us, we praise him for who he is: the God of love and mercy. The proclamation of the Gospel, teaching, Marian devotion, veneration of the Cross, Exposition and Benediction of the Most Blessed Sacrament, and our prayers of petition all lead us to praise. We know of God's mighty works throughout history and the unsurpassed love with which he has saved us. We trust that his grace is at work here and now—in our times and in our lives.

Praise the Lord

Praise the Lord, all nations!
Extol him, all peoples!
For great is his steadfast love toward us;

    and the faithfulness of the Lord endures for
        ever.
Glory be to the Father and to the Son and to
    the Holy Spirit,
As it was in the beginning, is now, and ever
    shall be, world without end.
Amen.

Laudate Dominum

Laudate Dominum omnes gentes,
laudate eum, omnes populi.
Quoniam confirmata est super nos
    misericordia eius
et veritas Domini manet in aeternum.

Gloria Patri et Filio et Spiritui Sancto.

Sicut erat in principio et nunc et semper et in
    saecula saeculorum.
Amen.